Yes Dear!
A Husband's Guide to Marriage

-by Joel Dubin

Acknowledgements

I want to thank my dear wife, Sara Guralnick, for her love and support in writing this book.

In fact, this book was her idea, and she suggested I write it based on our own humorous experiences and those of other married couples we know.

And, yes, in the spirit of this book, she was right.

> This is a humor book and in no way should be construed as actual marriage advise or counseling.

This is a work of fiction. Names, characters, places, and incidents are either the product of the author's imagination or are used fictitiously, and any resemblance to actual persons, living or dead, business establishments, events, or locales is entirely coincidental.

Copyright © 2021, 2024 Joel Dubin

All rights reserved.
No part of this book may be reproduced or transmitted in any form or by any means without written permission from the author.

ISBN-13: 9798990848610

About the Author

Joel Dubin is a retired cybersecurity consultant turned humor author. This book is inspired by his thirty-year-plus happy marriage to Sara Guralnick, also known as Queen Sara, the reigning monarch of the house. When not attending to her royal duties, Queen Sara is a children's book author. Dubin is the author of another humor book, The 7 Habits of Highly Dysfunctional Companies, based on his decades of consulting work with screwed up companies around the globe. He is a fluent in several languages and concluded that messed up companies have the same seven habits in every language. No longer banging his head against the wall with dysfunctional companies, he and Queen Sara live in Chicago.

Marriage is like waffles. You burn the first few before you get it right.
-- An Attorney in Chicago

YOU'RE WRONG!

YES, DEAR!
YOU'RE RIGHT, DEAR!

Table of Contents

Introduction 1

Pre-Marital: Training Camp 7

Marriage Pillar 1: Living Arrangements .. 20

Marriage Pillar 2: Shopping 34

Marriage Pillar 3: Chores 46

Marriage Pillar 4: Romance 56

Marriage Pillar 5: Sex 61

Afterthoughts 67

Introduction

The tips in this little guide book will save your marriage and that of countless others. Both husbands-to-be, and current husbands, will learn the true secret of marital bliss:

Keep Your Wife Happy

This book will get you, the husband, through even the most difficult situations in your marriage. This assumes, of course, there will be difficulties. There shouldn't be any rough patches, however, since you and your wife, like other happy couples, have probably already worked out all your differences before deciding to get married.

In the unlikely event a problem arises, you can refer to this book for help. You can carry this book with you at all times and pull it out at a moment's notice. Whatever you do, resist the urge to yell. Keep calm and reach for this book. This book is better than yelling. If you have to throw something, use the hand not holding this book. Make sure to duck if your wife throws something back. Don't let her grab hold of this book. She might throw it away. It's your marital life-saver.

If you can't carry this book in your back pocket, you can always hide it in a secret corner of your Man Cave. This is one of the few spaces in the house where the husband is allowed. Details are in the chapter, Living Arrangements.

Living arrangements finalized, restrictions and off-limits areas demarcated, you will need to fill your, actually, her (to be explained fully in Living Arrangements) new home with stuff. Furniture and flooring are only half the picture. You will have to make sure your wife has enough clothes and shoes. She should have more than she could ever wear in a lifetime. The house should be full from top to bottom. Techniques on keeping your wife clothed and not barefoot are in the chapter, Shopping. Defensive shopping techniques are also covered here.

Besides shopping, you must be prepared to be assigned endless chores and errands. These duties must be completed for your marriage to be running on all cylinders. Details of what is expected are in the chapter, Chores. Time management skills for chores are also included.

When shopping and chores have been completed, there may be time left for romance, covered in the chapter, Romance. If the husband builds up enough points – the point system is explained fully in the chapter, Sex – he might even get lucky. This isn't a given, but just in case, this chapter has pointers on getting ready for steamy – maybe not steamy – at least, lukewarm, encounters.

To recap, this book covers the five pillars of marriage:

1. *Living arrangements*
2. *Shopping*
3. *Chores*
4. *Romance*
5. *Sex*

One note of caution: You shouldn't be concerned about losing your identity in the marriage. You will still be identified as "the husband," "domestic servant," "the errand boy," "hopelessly in love," "starry-eyed" or just plain "hen pecked". You may lose your name, however. Yes, your wife may take your last name. But you will lose your full name. Others may refer to you as just "him".

It works this way. You and your wife are out somewhere. People will naturally gravitate to the center of power, your wife. She will introduce herself as "Mrs. So-and-so," and point at you. "I'm with him." When asked your name, you should say, "I'm him." Don't worry, if they look confused. Sooner or later, after they read this book, they'll figure it out.

This leads to the second secret of marital success:

She Is Always Right

There may be rare moments when you're right. They will help carry you through the rest of the time when you're wrong.

In those brief moments when you're right, she will be quiet. She won't admit you're right, and she is wrong. She won't have to wait long. These moments are fleeting – usually less than a day – and the ship will right itself naturally and get back on course. She will be back to being right – and you wrong – and will start talking again.

This book will prepare the husband for a life of always being wrong.

You need to remember these three rules:

Rule #1: She is always the boss.
Rule #2: She is always right.
Rule #3: See Rules #1 and #2 above.

Boundaries established, dating over, it's time to get down to the serious business of marriage. No more Routine Girlfriend Maintenance (RGFM) activities. Forget the flowers and the cards. No more cute gifts. Going out? Doing fun things? That's all over. It's TV at home together. Marriage is a permanent date. You're together for good. You're stuck.

One more note. This book isn't about High Maintenance Family Units, or children. It's only about the happy couple – you and your wife.

Hopefully, with this book, your marriage won't end up being another burnt waffle

First, before the fun and games of marital bliss, it's off to pre-marital training where the starry-eyed marital recruit meets reality.

Pre-Marital: Training Camp

After passing a psychological evaluation to determine mental fitness for marriage, the eager prospective husband must now undergo extensive basic training at a pre-marital boot camp. This training includes mental and physical preparation for the rigors of marriage. The recruit will also learn marital martial arts for navigating any domestic situation.

Over the entrance to the camp is a huge sign that says, "You're Wrong!". In fact, these signs are posted around the camp, except for a few "She's Right!" signs here and there to mix things up.

Attendees live in military-style barracks in austere conditions packed together in bunk beds. Next to each bed is a small chest, where only a few items of clothing, a couple of pairs of shoes and toiletries can be stored. This will prepare the prospective husband for the space restrictions, particularly closet space, he will face at home once married. He will only be allowed to keep a few items at home, just like at the camp during training. He will learn to feel lucky to be allowed even a toothbrush and comb.

The daily routine, just like married life, is fairly regimented. The prospective husband will learn to take orders and how to follow instructions. Also, just like the military, he will know his exact place in the marital hierarchy – at the bottom.

Each day starts promptly at five in the morning with the sergeant coming in and yelling, "Take out the garbage." Sleepy recruits will scramble to get out of bed, trying carefully not to bump into each other, stuffing garbage into bags put alongside their beds overnight.

After garbage duty, the sergeant yells out, "Fall in," and the prospective husbands gather into formation. This is the most crucial part of the day. They march shoulder-to-shoulder around the base for several hours, chanting, "YES DEAR".

To avoid monotony and keep spirits up, new chants are thrown in:

YES DEAR, NO DEAR
NO DEAR
OF COURSE, DEAR
OF COURSE NOT, DEAR
YOU'RE RIGHT DEAR
WHAT WAS I THINKING? DEAR
GREAT IDEA, DEAR

And then, the ultimate in groveling:

I SHOULD HAVE KNOWN BETTER THAN TO QUESTION YOUR JUDGMENT, DEAR

Notice all these chants end in "DEAR". This is on purpose. It adds a hint of affection and reminds the prospective husband he does everything for love. These chants are also sporadically broadcast throughout the day on loudspeakers around the camp, drumming them into the head of the marital recruit.

The sergeant will randomly yell at the men, "Are there any questions?" By this time, after long hours of drilling, the recruits are exhausted, and usually have nothing to say. The sergeant then yells, just like their future wives will do, "YOU'RE WRONG."

The prospective husband is surrounded all day, wherever he goes, by messages of negative reinforcement required for surviving his upcoming marriage.

Marching exercises now over, the afternoon is reserved for hard physical training in marital martial arts.

Shoe Store Defensive Maneuvers

As the prospective recruit will soon learn, his wife must have more shoes than an army. It is his mission to prevent, and block, shoe purchases as much as possible.

In this exercise, the recruit is placed inside a simulated shoe store. It has shoe displays, fully stocked shelves and shoe boxes scattered around the floor.

The recruits are camouflaged in shiny patent leather outfits and spread out throughout the store. Their faces are striped with black shoe polish war paint. A highly armed and dangerous salesperson, carrying a shoe horn and a measuring stick, is moving about the store. Their mission is to gather as many shoes as possible, staying ahead of the moving salesperson, put them back in their boxes and replace them on the shelves.

Recruits may have to crawl on the floor, going under shelves and stools, to get to the shoe boxes. Anybody in the way, attempting to try on shoes will have their shoes forcibly removed and repackaged in their boxes. The recruit must then carry the rescued shoe boxes and put them back in their place on the shelf. This is also known as the Shoe Box Closure and Return.

Dress Aisle Blocking Maneuver

Equally mystifying to husbands is the large quantity of clothing their wives must have. The Dress Aisle Blocking Maneuver is designed to slow, if not, stop this unnecessary accumulation.

The recruits enter the front door and fan out through the aisles. In this maneuver, the recruit blocks the aisle, bends slightly at the knees, crouching down, with elbows pointed out. It's important that the elbows stretch across the entire width of the aisle to block any ingress or egress.

Dress Aisle Sweeping Maneuver

It's not enough to just block the aisle. It also now needs to be cleared of shoppers, especially the wife. It needs to be swept and secured. Once the aisle is blocked, the prospective husband should advance swiftly to sweep the territory to push the wife aside. The husband needs to move fast enough to create a buffer zone between her and the racks. This should create a safe distance to keep her from reaching for more clothing. (See Figure 1.)

Figure 1
Note elbows spanning width of entire aisle for blocking maneuver.
Legs bent to allow swift movement down the aisle during the sweeping maneuver.

If his wife should still persist, then he'll need to pull out the ultimate weapon, the Anti-Shopping Puppets.

Anti-Shopping Puppets

This is a gentle maneuver, requiring more skill and finesse than other maneuvers. The recruits will break up into pairs, with one being the husband and the other the wife. The person in the role of the wife pushes a shopping cart.

The husband stands immediately behind the wife and extends his arms forward across the wife's ears. He then makes finger puppets with his hands. As the wife moves forward, the husband follows behind, moving his fingers, saying, "I don't need that. I already have one. No, I can't buy that." The idea is to implant subliminal messages to stop the wife from shopping. (See Figure 2.)

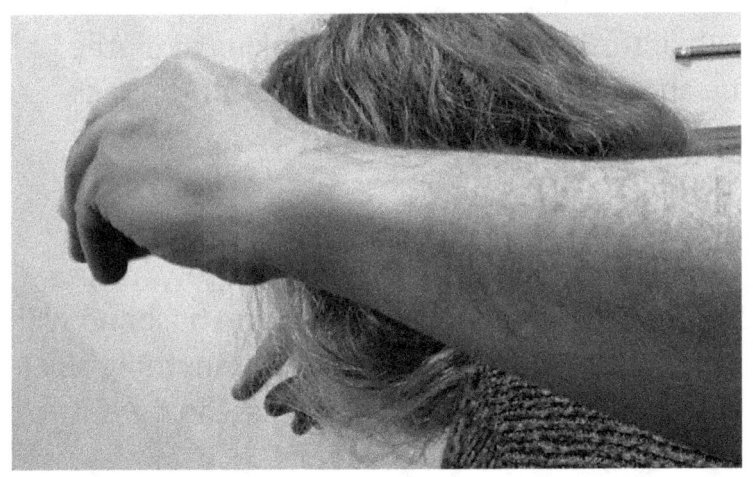

Figure 2
Note the husband's finger puppets giving subliminal messages directly into the wife's ears.

If that fails, and it usually does, since the wife will simply ignore the husband and maybe kick him out of the way, then extreme measures should be taken.

Shopping Cart Jamming

Horrified, as piles of clothing and stuff fill up the shopping cart, the husband will have to engage in guerrilla warfare: jamming the shopping cart.

While the wife is distracted looking at clothes, he should grab an empty hanger off the rack and surreptitiously jam it into a wheel of the shopping cart.

Unable to move the shopping cart toward the cashier, the wife will panic and the husband will say, "Honey, I guess we can't buy anything since the shopping cart is stuck and we can't get it to the cashier."

To be effective, this may need to be combined with strategic use of the Dress Aisle Blocking Maneuver. This depends, of course, on the placement of the shopping cart in the aisle.

Mailbox Lunge

Another source of shopping is mail order. The intrepid wife won't be deterred by staying at home. There are so many things to buy online or through a catalogue. The husband's mission is to block these catalogues from ever getting to the wife.

A simulated mailbox is set up in a field at the camp for this exercise. The recruit watches the mailbox with binoculars, and as soon as the mailman arrives, lunges forward and grabs the mail. He sifts through it ferociously, destroying any catalogues. When asked, he tells the wife there wasn't any mail for her today.

Errand Track

The recruit will be taught in basic training the most important role of the husband is to run arrands for their wives.

For this training, a series of errands and activities are set up at intervals along a track at the camp. At one station, there is a light bulb and a socket, where the bulb must be screwed on. At another, there is a hammer and a nail and a vertical board meant to be a wall. The nail must be hammered into the board, before moving on to the next station. There are also electrical plugs to plug in, dishes to be washed, household items to be fixed and toilets to be cleaned.

Finally, at the last station, there are 100-pound bags of rocks, meant to simulate shopping bags full of merchandise. Just beyond that is a parked car with the trunk open. In this activity, called the Shopping Bag Carry Maneuver, the recruit must carefully carry the heavy bags, careful not to break anything, and get as many as possible into the car trunk.

As the prospective husband will soon find out, post-shopping trunk stuffing is a key requirement to a happy marriage.

The sergeant will be standing at the end of the errand track, yelling: "That's not what I wanted. We have to go back to the store and exchange it."

Once the training is concluded, the formally confident single man will have been transformed, and broken down, into a malleable married husband ready to take orders and follow instructions without question.

He will have learned the following:

1. *The chain of command in the household with the wife as boss.*
2. *How to correctly tell the wife she is right.*
3. *How to follow instructions accurately.*
4. *How to handle shopping situations.*

The husband has successfully completed the basic training and is ready for marriage. The next hurdle will be living arrangements.

Marriage Pillar 1: Living Arrangements

Whoever said, "A man's home is his castle," didn't understand the basic principle of marriage: "A married man is a guest in his own home." It doesn't matter who legally owns the home, or whose name is on the title, it's hers. It's that simple.

The wife is the housekeeper in more ways than one. And, if she isn't the housekeeper, literally, meaning she has outsourced her chores to a cleaning lady, she still keeps the house.

Every husband knows that at any moment, he could be removed from the house. He could be replaced by a piece of large furniture – particularly a curio cabinet for all her tchotchkes – or moved into the hall or even put outside in a dog house. In fact, the family dog may be wondering why his father (the wife is also the dog's master, under the ownership rule mentioned above) is spending so much time with him.

The husband should just be grateful he's even allowed in her house, at all.

The husband has certain obvious living restrictions. First, the living room is off limits. It should really be called the "unliving" room, since no one lives there. The living room is strictly a display area, a showcase, if you will, of untouched furniture. It should be roped off like a room in a museum. In extreme cases, the wife may even wrap everything in plastic covers, so human hands don't touch the furniture.

Trespassing in the living room by the husband is a serious offense punishable by forced extra shopping trips up to and including the withholding of sex by the wife.

Just like plastic furniture covers, the wife will also want to put plastic runners covering the carpets in the hallways. The runners should be placed throughout the house. She will insist no shoes be worn in the house. Shoes must be left at the front door and be replaced by little disposable shoe guards. Heaven forbid human feet should touch the floor of her house (again, it can't be emphasized enough, it's her house, not his).

No less severe are restrictions in other parts of the house.

All closet space belongs to the wife. The husband is only allocated a single closet, usually the smallest one in the house, or part of a closet, no more. If he wants more closet space, he'll need to apply for a building permit.

Often the closets are jam packed with clothes and shoes, and even purses or other accessories. When the wife opens a closet, clothes bursting out, she may say, "I have nothing to wear." The husband should respond, "Then wear nothing."

This condition, known as the Packed Closet Appears Empty Syndrome, where the wife perceives a full closet to actually be empty, manifests itself in desires by the wife to go shopping, yet again. It's more important to accumulate than to use. The more clothing, even if unworn, the better. Another related phenomenon is the Still Price Tag Effect. Upon careful inspection, some of the clothes bulging out of the closet will still have price tags. These clothes, of course, can't be worn, thus necessitating another trip to the store for clothes to actually wear.

Shoes are a similar affair.

The wife can never have too many shoes. Maybe, she's afraid of being caught barefoot, despite owning thousands of pairs of shoes. As with clothing, the wife never has the right shoe, so has to buy another pair for each occasion, even if that occasion is to just go outside and get the mail. Picking up the mail is really the husband's duty but, on occasion, the wife may condescend to help the servants.

Also, as with clothing, shoes aren't always meant to be worn. Some will, of course, be worn. Others can be kept in their original box and shopping bag and just put away in a closet or a drawer. The price tag doesn't even need to be removed. Unworn shoes are a shopping trophy, proudly possessed and only displayed at appropriate times for friends and family.

Then there are purses and other accessories.

Here, again, some will be used, some will be stored. They're often kept together with shoes in closets. Some purses are works of art, not really designed to even hold anything. Why the wife buys them is a mystery to the husband. But buy them, they must. Otherwise, there are consequences.

The question of which will be worn, and which will be stored, is one of those great secrets of the marital universe. Some tchotchkes will survive, others may perish. Scholars have been unable to answer this question for thousands of years. The answer may never be known, not even to the wife.

Eventually, this accumulation of stuff comes with a price – beyond that charged on the credit cards – in terms of space. The wife asks herself whether she should seize more of the husband's already restricted space, have him move into the hall, or just throw him out of the house altogether to make room.

There are three options:

1. Buy another house just to store all the wife's things.
2. Get storage space or even rent a warehouse.
3. Retrofit the existing closets.

The most cost-effective way is to retrofit the closets. Closets can be converted into shoe and purse warehouses, rivaling the largest freight terminal in an airport. For shoes and purses, this can be done with extra shelves and rotating shoe racks. For clothing, multi-hangers that convert a single hanger, normally meant to hang only a single dress, into one holding five outfits.

The space expanding possibilities of spinning closets and overpacked hangers is mind-boggling. (See Figure 3.)

Figure 3
A closet packed with shoes and purses accumulated from shopping. This is an example of a well-arranged closet – shoes on one side, purses on the other. Note the price tags still attached to some of the purses on the right.

This just covers the wife's things. What about the husband's stuff? Since his space allowance is already severely restricted, this isn't a question. Whatever is left over, no matter how small, is his.

The wife should control the husband's apparel inventory in any case. She does this by attaching bar codes and color-coded tags to his clothing.

Some husbands are unable to dress themselves without their wife's assistance and will need the tags to match up appropriate outfits. The husband can't be allowed to sneak out of the house in the morning without a clothing inspection from his wife.

It's important to avoid the embarrassing situation where the husband goes to work with mismatched clothing, or outfits not approved by his wife, and someone in the office sees him and says, "Clearly, your wife didn't dress you today."

One suggestion the husband can make to reduce clothing clutter is to build a bonfire in the driveway or parking lot of all her unused clothing. The husband should make careful note of the wife's reaction to this idea.

The closets safely packed; attention can be turned to the other crucial room in the house – the bathroom.

It's critical the wife have her own bathroom. If she doesn't, the happy couple will have to share a single bathroom. That means, the husband will have no bathroom. There just won't be enough room for his few things. He won't be able to shave, shower or freshen up, let alone pee or poop, at all, inside the house. He'll be outside, again, with the already confused family dog.

The contrast between the two bathrooms is striking. The wife's bathroom is stocked with more cosmetics, skin care products, lotions, creams and toiletries than a pharmacy. Hair sprays, gels and shampoos sit packed on a rack in the shower. Her bathroom has more chemicals than a college chemistry lab.

Lighted mirrors, eyebrow pluckers, and other small torture devices are scattered around the sink. Lingerie and night gowns may even be hanging on the chair next to the lighted vanity set. It looks like a spa packed into a closet.

The husband's bathroom, on the other hand, is quite stark. There may be a comb and a brush, a toothbrush, a razor and, maybe, a bar of soap and some hair shampoo. That's it.

If the husband ventures into the wife's bathroom, he may be shocked. Before they were married, he had no idea she had bodily functions. She poops, she pisses and she farts out in the open in front of him.

If she is embarrassed by her farts, the husband should always reply, "It's because you're in love," or "Marriage gives you gas." This will ease bathroom tensions.

Claims must also be staked to other less important rooms in the house – the kitchen and the recreation room.

The kitchen, well, that depends on who uses it and for what purpose. If the wife cooks, it's her domain. If she doesn't cook, but just orders in, the kitchen can be refurbished for further clothing and shoe storage. If the husband cooks, under the marital house ownership rules, she still owns the kitchen but will have to grant him an easement, so he can at least enter.

The recreation room is another restricted area. The husband is only allowed one television for watching his shows. Control of the remote, of course, remains in the hands of the wife. He must ask permission to watch a game or the news. This privilege, like everything else in the house, can be granted or taken away at any time.

As a rule, the wife's comfort comes first. If the wife's comfort is the husband's discomfort, so be it. He sleeps on the lumpy side of the bed, so she can be comfortable. He sits in the sun, so she can be in the shade. He walks through puddles, so she can stay dry. He gives up the umbrella in the rain, when they only have one.

He runs through the rain to get the car to pick her up, so her shoes don't get wet.

Sleeping arrangements can also be tricky. It's probably a good idea to staple the sheets and linens to the mattress. This prevents a nocturnal tug-of-war over bed covers. Otherwise, the husband may end up completely exposed in the middle of the night. He may wake up to find all the sheets wound around the wife's leg. Slowly, throughout the night, she has been spinning the sheets around her leg until there is nothing left.

In extreme cases, the wife may gradually slide over to her husband's side of the bed, pushing him over to the edge little by little. The husband may find he is cramped into a sliver of the bed. Unless he takes swift and decisive action, he may get pushed out of the bed altogether. If she has also covered her pillows in towels to protect them from her face cream, the bed could be like an icy road. The husband could slip out of bed altogether. One solution – bars on the husband's side of the bed, just like in jail.

If the married couple makes it to middle age, and the wife starts having temperature issues, she may want to turn down the temperature in her house. She may want the air conditioning turned on even in the winter. As with everything else related to living together, the husband will have to be resigned to living in an ice box. If he tries to adjust the thermostat, she'll be right behind him to change it back.

The only exception to the normal living arrangements is the Man Cave. This is the only private space the wife allows the husband. It's usually the most inaccessible and uncomfortable part of the house, such as in the darkest corner of the basement. Here, the husband can do whatever he wants. It's his holy sanctuary. He can sit in his easy chair and smoke cigars, drink beer, watch sports and stain the carpet. He can crush cans and not be worried about missing the garbage can. It's his masculine canvass to dirty up. It can get gross. The wife only enters at her peril. She might pass out from the smell.

The living arrangements settled; next the house needs to be filled with stuff. That's where shopping comes in.

Marriage Pillar 2: Shopping

Shopping is an essential ritual of marriage. The husband needs to be prepared to spend time and, especially, money on shopping junkets with his wife. This may come as a shock to the newly trained husband, who struggles over buying a five-dollar pair of socks. Not so his wife. She will think nothing of maxing out a credit card in an hour shopping spree.

That's why she has more than one credit card. In fact, one of her many purses is bulging with them. When one is charged up, it's on to the next one. An empty credit card is a sad credit card. Credit card usage is also a leading indicator of the wife's health. If balances are up, she's been feeling good. If down, she may be under the weather.

There are so many things to buy. There are stores, and catalogues. Too much is not enough. As she spins around like a whirling dervish in the store aisle, flinging clothing into an overflowing shopping cart, she doesn't think about where everything will go in the house. Space is no object. Already packed closets can always be packed even more. When those are filled, there is always storage.

At the end of the day, the couple's SUV may not be enough for the haul. A forty-foot high-cube container and a freight forwarder might be needed.

There are shoes and purses, figurines for the curio cabinet, jewelry and accessories, dishes and cutlery for the kitchen, sheets for the bed, furniture and carpeting for the whole house. And then there are pictures for the wall. Let no corner of the house be untouched. Let no space be empty. Let no cabinet be unfilled. Let no wall be bare. Let no part of the floor be visible.

Shopping is a contact sport fought with credit cards and check books. Discount coupons in hand, or on her mobile phone, she's ready for in-store combat. She's on a first-name basis with the salespeople who smile as she comes in.

Meanwhile, the husband's head is spinning as he follows her into a store. She's a VIP. He's a nobody. They don't even notice him. He never comes in by himself, and when he does, it's usually to buy one item – a cheap screwdriver, a rare pair of pants and a shirt, maybe a wallet, maybe one sock (two aren't necessary, and they don't even have to match).

Husbands don't shop. They buy. Like a laser guided missile, the husband goes straight to the item he is looking for. Let's say he wants a pair of shoes. He knows exactly which one and what size to buy. He goes directly to the shelf where it's located. He tries them on to make sure they fit, puts them back in the box and marches straight to the cashier. He pays and is out the door. Total shopping time: less than 10 minutes.

Once he gets home with his shiny new shoes, he needs to make some life-and-death decisions. Due to space restrictions at home, he must choose which shoes must live, and which must die. His wife will insist he throw out a pair of old shoes to make room for the new. Unlike the wife, the husband is only allowed a strict quota of shoes. Once the quota is exceeded, even by only one pair, another pair must go. The same goes for suits, shirts, pants and belts and, of course, socks and underwear, which are known to take a lot of space.

Back at the store, his wife, on the other hand, is greeted by the employees like a visiting dignitary. A brass band may even greet her. She may be offered a glass of champagne.

Her mission: compress the Time-Money Ratio. She must spend more money per hour than last time. She must cover as many stores in the neighborhood as possible. Eventually, the happy couple on a shopping spree will be known as the Economic Development Action Committee, greeted by local officials for propping up the local economy.

The wife also follows the Two Choice Rule. If there are two choices, the more expensive one prevails. This holds true not just in stores, but for all other purchases, for example, redecorating, services, house repairs and restaurants.

The wife follows strict guidance as part of the Happy Spouse Shopping Code:

Rule of Thumb for Shoes — She can never have too many. She should have more shoes than she could ever wear in her lifetime, even if she changed pairs several times a day.

Rule of Thumb for Purses -- They should range in size from small hand-held pocket clutches to semi-suitcases. Some are strictly for decoration and shouldn't be used at all, in fact, should never be taken out of the bag after purchase, just stored in the closet. Possession is more important than use. It's the thrill of the shopping experience that counts. It's all about being out in the fresh air, and going around town.

Rule of Thumb for Jewelry – If the husband has to take out a second mortgage to buy it, go for it.

In the unlikely event the wife forgets her credit card or check book – a rare unprepared wife – she can summon her husband. "I just bought this. Go pay for it."

Between bouts of shopping, the wife must limber up. Calisthenics and weight lifting are good exercise for strengthening those arm muscles for faster credit card swiping and for lifting heavier shopping bags.

The wife must be properly attired for shopping. A mink coat is acceptable as long as it's loose fitting and doesn't prevent reaching shelves or dress racks. Shoes should be comfortable to allow for easily moving through the store. High heels are uncomfortable, and running shoes are unfashionable. A pair of flats allows the wife to glide down the aisles, quickly turn corners and effortlessly sweep through the whole store. (See Figure 4.)

Figure 4
Ideal shoes for the wife's shopping outing. Comfortable to allow easy movement, yet still stylish to show she is a real shopper – not just browsing – and out for serious spending.

In competitive situations, where there's a cluster of aggressive wives, maybe playing tug-of-war over a shoe on a discount table, a helmet and elbow-padding should be worn. This protects the wife when elbowing other nasty wives out of the way.

The wife must never be allowed to go shopping alone. She must always be accompanied by her shopping chaperone – the husband. Left alone in a store, she will run amok, not to be seen again for hours or days. She may use a clever ruse to escape. "Honey, I'm just going in for one thing." If the husband isn't paying attention, she could disappear into a black hole, only to be rescued when the credit card has reached its limit or the shopping cart tips over from being overloaded.

The modern husband is an active participant in shopping. He should ask every five minutes, "Are we done yet?" If asked, which isn't often, whether she should buy a particular item, the husband should cleverly reply either, "Does it cost more than five dollars?" (this is a good question when she asks about expensive jewelry) or "The answer is no. What's the question?"

If the husband dares to interfere in her shopping, by saying, for example, "Why are you buying another pair of shoes?" the salesperson may tell him to go away. "Who asked you?" Meddling husbands are bad for business.

Gone are the days when husbands could be seen gathered at meeting points in the store, reading newspapers, while their wives shopped. The husbands would never talk to each other – that would be unacceptable and violate spousal shopping etiquette. The husbands had an unspoken understanding. They were all part of the same secret fraternity – Husbands of Shopping Wives. Many, hungry and tired, used to wait for hours for their wives to return to pick them up.

The husband must try to fight back against the shopping folly. His first line of defense is the too small shopping cart. In this defensive maneuver, he deftly enters the store first, just ahead of his wife, grabs the smallest shopping cart available and takes control of the first stage of the shopping operation.

His objective in the operation code named, Reduce Spending, is to try to limit her purchases. He does this first by reducing the shopping collection space with the smallest vehicle possible.

When the cart is full, he proudly declares, "Dear, the cart is full. We can't buy anything else. We have to check out." The wife is usually wise to this maneuver and says, "Then get a bigger cart, Honey."

At this point, the husband has to call out the heavy artillery – the tactics he learned in basic training:

- Shoe Store Defensive Maneuvers
- Dress Aisle Blocking Maneuver
- Dress Aisle Sweep Maneuver
- Anti-Shopping Puppets
- Shopping Cart Jamming

Another fun idea is the Credit Card Challenge. The husband sends his wife on a weekend getaway with nothing but the clothes on her back and a credit card in hand. Her goal: She must charge her way out of the situation. As soon as she gets off the plane, she will have to rent a car or get a taxi or ride service, and book a hotel, find places to eat and find her way around town. She will need to buy a suit case (or several to bring back her bounty) and clothes for the weekend, then it's out to do what she loves to do most: shopping.

When she comes back, he shouldn't be surprised when a delivery truck comes to the door, asking where to unload the pallets of merchandise.

One area of shopping best left for the husband is groceries. This isn't really considered shopping, since it's a chore, and chores are the husband's responsibility. If the husband has to be uncomfortable, so his wife can be comfortable, then she should rest comfortably at home, while her husband does the groceries.

Here, too, there are certain rules. The wife, as with everything else in the husband's life, still has the final say in the matter. First, the husband should always be sent with a grocery list. Husbands without lists are clueless and will have no idea what to buy.

Husbands without grocery lists are also a security threat in the store. They wander aimlessly up and down the aisles and could be mistaken for shoplifters, prompting calls to store security. The list should have the wife's phone number. This way, the confused husband can hand the list to a store clerk and grunt. The clerk can call the wife to find out what she really wants.

If the husband brings home the wrong thing, he may be severely reprimanded, at best, or sent to the dog house, again, at worst.

Whatever the wife brings home from her shopping, even if it's the ugliest white elephant tchotchke, the husband must accept. "Isn't it beautiful," she says, placing it on a table already packed with other hideous items.

The husband must reply with the only answer he knows: "Yes, Dear!"

Marriage Pillar 3: Chores

To the wife, the husband is a live-in servant and errand boy. As he learned in pre-marital training, he is expected to be on call for his wife 24x7. He is expected to be at her beck and call for even her craziest whim at any hour of the day and night. The only biological function of husbands is to run errands and carry stuff for their wife. They serve no other purpose.

Every husband knows his job is to follow instructions.

Whether or not the wife works is irrelevant. She doesn't believe her husband really works. The wife believes he is on call, and only for her, even at work. He is supposed to be sitting by his desk, waiting for her call at any moment to take care of something. Who else is he working for, other than his wife? It's important the husband makes his supervisor at work understand he is second in command after his wife. He needs to explain to his supervisor that his real boss is his wife and, of course, she, and her orders, always come first. He actually reports first to his wife, then to his supervisor.

The husband then has two bosses – his work boss and his home boss, his wife, the real one.

The properly indoctrinated husband may spontaneously blurt out in the office at random times, "Yes, Dear!", while sitting at his desk. His neighboring unmarried co-workers will wonder what is going on. The married men, on the other hand, will understand immediately, since they're all in the same situation. Some may smile or wave, or even wink back at him in acknowledgement.

The husband needs to exercise enough self-control in the office to make sure he doesn't accidentally say "Yes, Dear!" to his supervisor. It could be very embarrassing.

When the wife calls, the husband must suddenly stop what he is doing and answer the phone.

The conversation may go something like this:

Wife: "I have something to tell you."
Husband: "You're madly in love with me."
Wife: "No, nothing like that."
"Could you please pick up some bread on the way home?"
Then she just hangs up.

Many wives complain their husbands don't listen. This may be true. Studies have shown that the Husband Hearing Ratio is forty to fifty percent, at best. That means the husband only hears every other word. Key parts of the wife's instructions may be missed.

If the husband isn't even listening, how can the wife communicate instructions? One answer is a service animal, a Hearing Ear Dog, the audio counterpart to a Seeing Eye Dog.

The best way, then, is for the wife to not communicate verbally at all with her husband. She should use non-verbal cues, such as snapping her fingers or using hand signals, like semaphore flags or Morse code. A quick flip of the wrist one way means one thing ("Take out the garbage!"), while a slight gesture another way could mean something entirely different ("Take me shopping now."). Whistling has also been known to be effective.

If the wife snaps her fingers – the most popular way to summon the husband – she might say something like, "Come here, Dear. I need you for something." This is the husband's cue to come over immediately. He instinctively knows she doesn't "need" him for sex right now (maybe later). That would get in the way of the endless household chores on her list.

The following is a small, though not exhaustive, list of possible chores expected of the husband:

- *Take out the garbage*
- *Fix the toilet*
- *Clean the kitchen*
- *Take me shopping*
- *Get the groceries*
- *Put in a light bulb*
- *Take me shopping*

- *Make me breakfast*
- *Make me breakfast in bed*
- *Take me to the hairdresser*
- *Do the laundry*
- *Take me shopping*
- *Do the dishes*
- *Fix this, fix that*
- *Move this piece of furniture*
- *Take me shopping*
- *Take the dog out*
- *Mow the lawn*
- *Take me shopping*
- *Take me to breakfast*
- *Take me shopping*
- *Take me to lunch*
- *Take me to dinner*
- *Take me shopping*
- *Take me shopping*

Note that "let's have sex" isn't on the list. This is a special chore, covered in depth in its own chapter, since it requires special tools and methods. Also note the prominence of repeated requests for "Take me shopping". This shouldn't come as a surprise to the experienced husband.

Cooking is a tricky subject. If she does cook, and enjoys it, the issue is settled. If she is of royal lineage, as some wives consider themselves, cooking is problematic. It could ruin her nails. The heat in the kitchen might make her hair droop, or make her makeup run.

In that case, the wife will do the next best thing – send her husband for carry out. She is a culinary magician with the phone or online. This is the modern equivalent of prehistoric man going hunting, fishing and trapping for food. Clearly, nothing has changed since the dawn of time.

The husband should be kept in a constant state of motion. He shouldn't be allowed to rest. When a task is successfully completed, he should be given a tasty treat, like a dog. If he messes up a task, the wife should roll up a newspaper and say, "Bad husband. Stand in the corner." In any case, when a task has been completed, successfully or not, he should be assigned a new one right away. The new task should be assigned as soon as possible, just in time to keep him from sitting in his favorite chair or, worse yet, before returning to his Man Cave, where he might not be seen again for hours.

Sending the husband out alone on an errand, can also be dicey. First, he must be properly attired before being allowed to leave the house. Many husbands can't dress themselves correctly. The clever wife will put color coded tags on the husband's few clothes, so he can put together matching outfits.

The husband needs to understand that if anyone asks him question during an errand, he must say he isn't authorized to answer questions. He has to call home first. "I have to clear this with headquarters."

The best way to avoid potential situations with a husband out of the house, is to have the wife accompany him.

The fully trained husband is the wife's chauffer. They have to use his car. She won't allow her car out of the garage. Under the Two-Car Rule, the wife gets the nicer of the couple's two cars but doesn't drive it. If there is only one indoor parking space, it's hers. He parks outside in the cold and heat, and the snow and rain. Her car is only for show or for bragging to her friends that she has a luxury car.

Once on the road, the wife becomes the co-pilot. She gives him directions, and points out items of interest on the road. She may even direct traffic, yelling obscenities at cars that cut them off, or pointing out other bad behavior by passing cars. If the husband makes a wrong turn, she asks him why he went out of the way, and then will hit him on the shoulder. This is supposed to scare him into driving better.

The car is no different than being at home. The husband doesn't pay attention to what the wife says. As with other instructions, he also ignores her when driving.

This leads the husband to take wrong turns. He may get off at the wrong exit. He may space out altogether and be on auto-pilot, driving without thinking to some place he normally goes, like the golf course or a sports stadium, maybe even his favorite bar with the guys. He should especially avoid accidentally ending up at the guys' favorite titty bar. The wife might raise some unpleasant questions. The wife must be alert to keep him on the right path. She must ignore him, when he says, "I know where I'm going." Only she knows where they're going. Only she knows the secret path to their destination.

Besides offering expert driving tips, the wife is also the happy couple's Social Director. She is in charge of making all plans. If someone asks the husband what he is doing for the weekend, he usually replies, "I have no idea. Ask my wife." Only she knows their mission, and she isn't telling. Any attempt at scheduling anything through the husband is null and void and should be ignored. If he tries to make a date, the husband will screw it up anyways.

The husband should expect the wife to approach him at any time without advance notice to get dressed and ready to go out. "Shut up. Get dressed. You're wearing this. This is where we're going." The experienced husband won't be fazed at all by this. Being told to randomly get dressed at a moment's notice might have even been part of his pre-marital training. Unannounced activities by the wife are totally normal.

Whether in the house, or out of the house, in the car or on the road, the husband has his chores.

Marriage Pillar 4: Romance

After the heavy lifting of the marriage – shopping and chores – are done, there is time left for romance. These are some suggestions to keep those flames of passion burning.

Romance should start first thing in the morning. When the wife is just getting up, the husband should say, "How's my angelic vision of beauty?" This may be met with a screaming, "It's too early in the morning. Leave me alone." If she is wearing her "I don't do mornings" t-shirt, watch out. The love-struck husband should persist any ways. It can only get better as the day wears on.

Since the wife won't get out of bed voluntarily, the husband might as well serve her breakfast in bed. To make this look authentic, he should wear a butler outfit and bring her food on a tray. A white towel thrown over his arm, like a waiter at a high-end restaurant, is a nice touch.

He can even ask, "Would the madame like anything else?" It's not a good idea to light a candle in bed. It could be a fire hazard.

When the wife is getting dressed, she may ask, "Does this outfit make me look fat?" The husband should always reply, "No, dear. Not, at all. You look cute in that."

The husband should never respond, "I love you no matter how fat you are," or "That seam over there looks like it's about to burst." The consequences could be severe: loss of points, up to and including withholding of sex altogether for a while (see the chapter, Sex). It could also result in a forced penalty shopping spree, which could be very costly.

Finally, last but not least, are the wife's shoes. The husband should grab a pair of shoes, any shoes. It doesn't matter. There should be several nearby on the floor. Then he should put one on her foot and say, "It fits! Cinderella, I found you." If she doesn't whack him on the side of the head with the other shoe, he knows he made progress.

The husband should answer all questions with, "Because you're in love." If she gets indigestion from his cooking and wonders why she has gas and is belching, he should say, "Because you're in love." He should explain to her marriage gives you gas. Marriage is basically about intestinal compatibility. If they can't tolerate their food together, they won't stay together.

The husband may be prompted to say, "Because you're in love," in response to other bodily functions and feelings. The wife may ask, "Why am I peeing so much today?" The answer, of course, is "because you're in love." She asks, "Why does my dress itch?" Obviously, the husband says, "Because you're in love." "Why don't the shoes I just bought fit?" "Because you're in love."

Here's another great answer guaranteed to keep the romantic torch burning. The wife says, "I have something to tell you." The husband answers, "You're madly in love with me and can't think straight." The wife shoots back, "That wasn't it."

The romantic husband knows he must put his wife on a pedestal, even call her a Queen. He should tell people, even complete strangers, he married royalty. He is a mere peasant compared to his regal wife.

The Queen, of course, must have her throne. It could be the toilet in the bathroom, where she spends part of the day. It could even be her favorite piece of expensive furniture in the living room. It is from here she holds court. When the husband has made her angry, she reminds him she has beheaded others for less.

Outside the palace, the Queen is escorted by her valet service (meaning, her husband). When she is ready to be picked up and summons her husband, the husband must answer the phone, "Queen So-and-So's Valet Service. Is the queen ready to be picked up?" People overhearing may flinch. The husbands will understand. They know their role.

The husband is expected to pick up his wife, even if he has to run in the rain to get the car.

The Queen must stay dry. If there is only one umbrella, she gets it. Getting soaked in the rain to protect his wife is part of the romance of marriage.

Birthdays, anniversaries and national holidays, aren't just one day long. They're romantic – and spending – opportunities. Week-long shopping junkets are wrapped around each event. To the husband, the Queen's birthday and Christmas feel like they last all year long. The wife will remind the husband: Every day is Wife's Day.

These romantic tips should help the husband accumulate enough points towards his ultimate goal – getting laid.

Marriage Pillar 5: Sex

Sex must be carefully rationed. There can't be either too much or too little. The correct balance is difficult to achieve. However, there is a handy tool for determining the exact frequency of sex allowed in the marriage, and how much sex the husband should expect. Even with the tool, the husband has to put in a lot of effort to get his canoe shellacked.

Before diving into this miracle tool, it's important to understand the fundamental difference in how husbands and wives view sex.

The husband makes the mistake of thinking marriage is all about sex. He is all excited, thinking he will get laid all the time after getting married. He thinks the following:

1. Sex in the bedroom.
2. Sex in the bathroom.
3. Sex in the kitchen.

4. Sex all over the house all the time.

Little does he know the wife is really thinking:

1. We need a new bedroom set.
2. The bathroom needs remodeling.
3. We need new appliances in the kitchen.
4. The whole house actually should be redecorated.

In addition, some husbands may see sex as getting in the way of their golf game. Other husbands think foreplay is a half hour of begging.

This is a clear disconnect in the rules of engagement on the sexual battlefield.

The best way to resolve this paradox is the Beaver Point System (BPS), in which points are generated and then deposited in a Beaver Bank (BB). At a certain point, the bank is full, and the points can be cashed out, sort of like credit card rewards points.

Here is how the little beaver system works:

Whenever the husband behaves well – successfully completes an errand without smashing up the car, buys the wife an expensive bauble, keeps quiet, and actually listens while the wife is talking, etc. – the bank is credited with beaver points. Whenever the husband behaves badly – fails to complete an errand, tries to contradict his wife, or worse, tells her she is wrong, attempts to take more closet space than allowed, tries to sit in the living room, tracks dirt into the house, etc. – points are deducted from the bank.

Obviously, the total points accumulated in the bank fluctuate every day, going up and down just like the stock market. Except gains or losses in the stock market don't translate into gains or losses of sexual opportunities. Beaver Points, on the other hand, can be exchanged for sex. There is a direct correlation between Beaver Points and sexual activity.

For example, eventually, if the husband plays his chips right, the Beaver Bank will fill up. When this happens, the lights in the house will start blinking, a disco ball with strobe lights will drop down from the ceiling and loud music – preferably heavy metal – will start playing. In exceptional cases, naked little angels blowing horns will fly overhead.

When the pumped in mist clears, the husband will see a vision. The wife will be standing there in slinky lingerie, apparently ready for action. The husband must tread carefully, otherwise he could lose beaver points and blow the whole thing. He can't tell her she looks like a sack of potatoes, even if she's put on a bit of weight recently. Instead, he must crouch down like a football player, grab her and throw her over his shoulder and head straight to the bedroom.

The husband must prepare his loins immediately for orgasmic battle and use whatever tools at his disposal – lubricants, erectile dysfunction pills, car jacks, air pumps, rubber bands, sex toys – to complete the act. Immediate and decisive action is necessary, since the husband never knows when this ship will come back into port.

Another pitfall the husband must avoid is yelling out the name of another women during sex. This could lead to more than just a drastic cut in beaver points.

Afterwards, the couple can share a smoke, knowing full well the Beaver Bank has been completely cashed out. Depleted and exhausted, the whole process to refill the bank must be started over from scratch. The husband is back to zero and must work to deposit Beaver Points back in the bank if he has any hope of ever having sex again.

Conversely, points can be deducted from the Beaver Bank for various transgressions. The list includes not following instructions, failure to pay for shoe purchases, breaking a piece of furniture and so on. Since the husband is by default always wrong, the list is endless.

When points are deducted, the husband's chances for sex diminish. If the points drop enough, like a stock market crash, the whole system comes to a halt. It's possible to have a negative balance in the Beaver Bank. When this happens, the wife will withhold sex until the balance is back in the black.

To sum up, Beaver Points are like doggy treats. The husband gets them for good behavior and loses them for bad behavior. As a result, it's critical for the husband to keep the balance in the Beaver Bank positive.

The Beaver Point System is a marriage-saver. It has brought many happy couples back from the brink of the sexual wilderness and into horny city.

Afterthoughts

Now that you've finished reading this book, you've fixed all the problems in your marriage. You can breathe a sigh of relief and pat yourself on the back.

How about calling each other by cute little pet names, like "Bunny" and "Muffin"? It doesn't matter who is the "Bunny" and who is the "Muffin." Each of you should just pick one, and see which sticks.

You've successfully navigated the five pillars of marriage and have created a happy home.

Here is a quick reference table as a reminder:

Living Arrangements	It's her house, and your space is restricted.
Shopping	Keep spending and filling up her house.
Chores	You are available at her beck and call 24x7.
Romance	Keep those flames of passion burning bright.
Sex	Keep collecting those points.

As long as you respect and support each other; as long as you listen to each other and are affectionate, love will carry you through.

But by all means remember what's important:

Always have fun together!

www.ingramcontent.com/pod-product-compliance
Lightning Source LLC
Chambersburg PA
CBHW050331010526
44119CB00004B/124